LAST RITES AND OTHER POEMS

David Citino

LAST RITES
and other poems

Ohio State University Press : Columbus

187579

Copyright © 1980 by the Ohio State University Press
All Rights Reserved.

Library of Congress Cataloguing in Publication Data

Citino, David, 1947
  Last rites and other poems.

  I. Title.
PS3553.I86L3   811'.54   80-14993
ISBN 0-8142-0314-0

FOR MARY

CONTENTS

ONE: THE SENTENCE

TWO: PLAGUE

THREE: HISTORIA NATURALIS

FOUR: THE TRIAL OF MARTHA CARRIER

FIVE: SITUATIONS

SIX: THE LIFE OF A SAINT

SEVEN: WHERE NO SON CAN EVER DIE

EIGHT: THE THING

ACKNOWLEDGMENTS

Grateful acknowledgment is made for permission to reprint here poems that have appeared, often in slightly different form, in various periodicals and anthologies.
"Mario Lanza Defeats Luciano Pavarotti in a Tenor Competition Held on a Turntable in My Father's Living Room" was first published in *Aspen Anthology*, No. 5 (1978); "The Trial of Martha Carrier" was published in the October 1976 issue of *Cimarron Review*, and is reprinted by permission of the Board of Regents for Oklahoma State University; "Situation No. 7: The Poison Lover" first appeared in *Descant* (Vol. 22, No. 4); "March 8: John of God" was first printed in *The Fiddlehead* (Fall 1979); "The Death of Ray Chapman" appeared in the Fall-Winter 1976 issue of *Hiram Poetry Review*; "Last Rites" is reprinted from *The Literary Review* (Vol. 22, No. 3, Spring 1979), published by Fairleigh Dickenson University; "Isaac" will appear in *The Pikestaff Forum #3*; and "Challenging Situation No. 3: The Rolling Skull" was published in *Red Cedar Review* (Vol. 11, No. 2 [1977]).
Other poems have appeared in *Anthology of Magazine Verse and Yearbook of American Poetry; Beloit Poetry Journal; Borestone Mountain Poetry Awards: Best Poems of 1976; Green River Review; The Hollins Critic; Hollow Spring Review of Poetry; James Joyce Quarterly; Kudzu; Long Pond Review; The Ohio Journal; Poet and Critic; St. Andrews Review; San José Studies; Discover America 1976: San José Studies Special Issue; Sequoia; Southern Humanities Review; Southern Poetry Review; The Sun: A Magazine of Ideas; West Branch; WIND/Literary Journal;* and *Wisconsin Review*.

ONE: THE SENTENCE

THE SENTENCE

That first spring
Cain fashioned stone into fence
and with his oxen trampled the earth
until it bled honey and grain
but his brother, whose scent
Cain couldn't abide,
rearranged the fence into stone
because his lambs couldn't understand it
and reddened their fleece
with the lack of understanding
so Cain shattered his brother
and sowed him over the fields
and scattered his sheep
and tried to wash his hands
but the scent was in his hair
and deep in his skin and when,
at harvest, Cain fired his first fruit
God flew down into his head
and shouted "Listen, when you burn
your fruit to do me honor
the stench of your brother
wafts through heaven like angry singing—
why is that?" And Cain couldn't answer
and walked out over the earth
with God's thumbprint on his head
to look for lost sheep and topple fences
and try to flee the din behind his eyes
and to this day when something burns
the smell of his brother covers heaven
and God hasn't let him die
and God hasn't stopped shouting.

LADDERS

If you lie in a field
where nothing's growing
late at night between rivers
with your hands touching stone
as the August wind
whispers its close myths
over your parts,
you'll dream a forest of ladders
between earth and sky
and burly angels
climbing, their arms
wrapped around
staring brittle ones,
or descending, arms
cradling sleeping babies,
with only constellations
and the flame inside your head
to show them the way up,
to light their way down.

DAUGHTER

Our father is old, and there is not a man
in the earth to come in unto us.

To the mirror, as to a sister,
when she saw dawn redden her lips
as it crept over her bare left shoulder
that day thirty-nine years
beyond her first dawn, she said
"He's grown gray as a lake
under a cloud of days, as stone,
stares out through the door
envying the forest's wet scent,
lonelier even than I, as he's male,
missing her more, as he must,
too fragile to endure under grass.
I'll prepare savory meat
crimson enough to quicken the blood
and too many cups of wine
for him to count
but not so many he can't remember
and become my beast in the fable of him
and his in the fable of me
and we'll go in to him
driven by blood and its music of must
and insinuate ourselves between his limbs
and take him back to where we begin,
a greedy boy we'll tutor and feed
until he hurts us with the human wound
and our bloods meet
between sleep and dream, and be to him
what it's our lot to be, nothing
and all, arms and legs open briefly,

then shut with regret, and later
touch his thigh and swear
long before the heavens rumble,
long before our bellies swell
to be there to close his eyes."

ISAAC

Hast thou but one blessing, my father?

It's true my eyes have dimmed
like a flame
with only moments left to burn
above the rising tide of wax,
and my lips and tongue have lost
their resolution, what once was taut
and disciplined now loosening
to petulance and little-boy whines,
face and hands shattering
from the weight of weeks,
like a winter sky seen through trees.

But slowed by age's plague as they may be,
my senses still hunger after love;
it wasn't only time
that made me confuse duty and affection,
venison and goat-meat
or the woman-skin of a young man's cheek
still fat with the beauty of the breast
and the leathered flesh of a man who stands
all day between his labor and the wind
and stinks like the herd and field
God's just blessed.

I knew the voice that loved me
out of darkness was too near its mother's,
the scent I wrapped my arms around
mingled with hers, contrived,
and yet I played the role of that father
hatred of decay makes foolish.
I've one blessing only, Esau—
he took it to your mother.
But you'll share the legacy my father
cursed me with, the law that makes us
hate and love our brothers.

MARY'S SECOND CHILD

Then Joseph . . . took unto him his wife: and knew her not till she
had brought forth her first born son. —Matthew

It's no miracle I'm what I am, believe me.
I was the harvest of a sweaty, human planting,
never far enough from the whine of father's saw.
No credulous beasts, no Eastern mystics
tired of gold or human boys heard my birth;
and where was I to find a winged heaven
to trumpet my entrance? I had no connections.

Mother worked to give me light,
her first curse my first lullaby.
If there was in her groaning a measure
of disappointment—even outrage—who could blame her?
The only men she knew before me or her husband
were angelic, everlasting and painless,
their bodies light as cloud.

Joseph grasped at what he couldn't comprehend,
shook his dusty hands at the sky, his lust
fed by the jeers of every young fool in town.
On the night he first touched her,
as much in anger as need, he told me later,
she lay looking at him as if she were
queen of heaven, and he grew soft as cloth.

But after what she'd been through
the first time, she was ready to see
in every pail of water drawn from the well
a shining dove hovering near her reflection,
in each wine cup or scrap of fish
an alien son, arrogant and cold.
Love held no more surprises for her.

When she died gray and confused
just before learning to fly
she looked at me, the image of her two lovers,
and called me "Jesus"—she's up there now
singing at him, most likely, beaming.
When you're conceived to walk with angels
can children of earth and flesh move you?

TWO : PLAGUE

PLAGUE

And in these days was burying without sorrowe
and wedding without friendschippe.

1.

In October the Genoese trader
pulls too slowly into Messina's harbor
to outrace the incense of last rites,
riding low in the water
with a treasure of eastern rats and fleas,
the men at the oars dark as pitch,
but not from sun, the aching in each groin
worse than any hurt that comes from love,
a swelling the size of an apple;
death draped around their shoulders
like an old mother's shawl.

2.

The seacoast towns would be the first
to recognize the smell
of what was washed ashore, and know
the sudden change that tide and wind
can bring in trade—portly men,
their fingers heavy with jewels,
slumping over in the counting houses
on scales fashioned to reckon
only the gravity of silver, salt and spice,
the going rate for Flanders cloth,
a tun of Rhenish wine. Too many
lost their fortunes trying
to bribe away the dark, not understanding
that for half the world to remain in daylight
the other half
must spend their lives in night.

3.

Soon churchyards swelled
to fill the cities with stone
and mounds of pungent earth, towns
climbed back into forest or fell into bog,
monasteries lying still as the Eucharist,
with no one left to till or reap
or glean the broken, bone-dry letters
of each name
to keep the flames of chronicle alive.

4.

Through China, India, Islam and Europe
man and flea and rat
ran in relay toward evening and the Atlantic
faster than the Mongol horsemen
in whose saddlebags it all began.

At each town and gristmill
death put down roots. Even when the people
were light enough on their feet to flee
they took with them the reason for flight,
insisting on cough or kiss
as they lay together on the last night
listening to the squealing of black rats
in the thatched roof above the bed,
the soft words in the language
of future alchemist and priest:
Pasteurella pestis.

5.

"From hell or heathen," wise men said;
holy ones ripped their flesh with whips
and sliced off ears and fingers
to sip the bright new sacrament,
stared at the sun and tried to learn again
to love a God who had to be malevolent or mad;
but the people knew the Plague Lady

came at night in dreams
to wrap her legs around theirs,
then flew from the dark one's mouth at dawn
in a flame blue as Mary's eyes
and ran next door to kiss
the neighbor's children on the lips;
they knew the Jews polluted each well
with the bloodless carcasses of Christian infants
and the same potent spells they'd used
to trap and kill a savior. They dragged them
from their synagogues
and threw them on bonfires
already tall from a century's quota
of blackened tooth and bone.

6.
Mothers and fathers
extinguished children
who began to lose their light,
priests and doctors hid in darkened houses
and refused the pleas
to come and shrive or bleed the poor;
pardoners stumbled on the roads
clutching bags of shillings, scapulars and sous,
their pockets fat with pieces of the cross,
twigs plucked from the burning bush,
vials of milk from the Virgin's breast.
In every street the living fell upon the living
stiff with rage or lusting, death's breath
hot on the backs of their necks,
firing cities into cinders, the future
shriveling to what can be remembered only,
lauds and matins of a million mornings
wafting toward heaven
in pillars of thick, foul smoke.

7.
With their yelps and the crack
of the spiked whips they pranced before,
they tried to startle the Black Death back

into sewer, granary and burrow,

as the blood that trickled
from their tattered flesh mothers
old before their time caught
on the family's finest cloth

to soothe a baby's blisters
or brew a resurrection stew.
They danced and danced because one night
a third of the world grew still

and what else can one do
when heaven grows so vengeful
but keep moving, offering to lightning bolt
and rat fang no easy target?

Maddened by the bite of the tarantula,
some said, or following in the steps of David,
Salome or young Saint Vitus, they drummed
their prayerful rhythms over Europe

skipping over smoldering corpses
light as sunrise on a brimming river
or flat stones flung from the shore,
bees dizzy with death's bitter nectar.

8.
Men had to learn all over
how to stand and walk and be both good and bad;
cities passed laws against wearing black
and shedding tears and going out and coming in.
In every castle, hut and cloister
the eyes of the dying burned clear in the eyes
of pale survivors, bodies rising
at first light from filthy straw, fleas
leaping from their limbs, to dance
around the floor, scythe in hand, the sounds
that issued from their darkened lips
a rasping chant:

I'm the way from A to Z,
the plowman, furrow, seed and bee;
dance all four ways with me,
thighs on mine, lips—
what reason can there be
for saying no when everyone
around seems senseless?

You're not old enough
or wise until you wake
from dream to find
in all the world
I'm the only one who can
be feared, the only one
who can't be. Look at me—

what I am is only you.

9.
The harbor master of Messina
boards the vessel swaying at anchor
under a silent sky, Genoa's banners
flapping from the mast.

A scarlet, scented scarf covering his nose,
the rosary wrapped three times around his hand,
a drumming in his chest and the inside
of his wrist, he studies the shadows
stretched out on the warped planks,
the madness rolling in the eyes, drooling
from the lips of the few
the darkness hasn't reached.
He's the first to realize
there'll be no place to hide.
He sees out of the corner of his eye,
then lightly at his feet, scurrying
over the polished buckle of his shoe,
the shadow of a rat.

THREE : HISTORIA NATURALIS

HISTORIA NATURALIS

Who could ever believe in the existence of the Ethiopians
who had not first seen them?—Pliny

In Atlantis
there lives a nation of warriors
invincible because
nothing grows between their legs.

The pleading screams of a virgin
facing heaven
whose knees are being forced apart
can summon hard rain and retribution.

Even dung ages to jewel;
snakeskin shivers into music
when spring wind whispers:
in time, all things grow lovelier.

The hyena learns the names of shepherds
and, calling them from the tent
at night in a young girl's voice,
devours the tongue and human parts,

impersonates the song of a man retching
to summon dogs and flies,
but scratches in a burial ground
to still the real hunger.

Races of wonder-folk cover the earth,
small as a baby's fist, large
as lust or thunder, men with parts
of bears, horses, ewes or elms,

those whose lips and tongue
have grown so parched with passion
there's no up or down, men
so far from women they live

to live inside them; women
who hunger to ride the serpent;
men who can be only below
or above the waist, women the same.

Those who need to see
merely what they see.

PROVERBS

A loose woman's a bottomless pit,
the deceiving man's
a ladder with a broken rung.

The beauty of a young man
lies between his legs, an old man's
behind his eyes, between his lips.

Hands can't hold or carry water
when they're fists.

A woman and man can't be driven apart
when their hands hold fast to one another,
when what they make of love
has two backs, eight limbs, one pulse,
when they move together to the same music.

Four things can't last forever:
a storm, a peaceful sky, a life, a love.

He who gives himself to love's
a tilled field in early spring;
who holds his neighbor in contempt's
a teeming city after dark.

As cold air to a broken tooth,
as a chancre to a lover,
so's death's grin to one who has no memories
of steamy nights in automobiles
in woods or near the sea, soft beds
in rooms fragrant and dim with late afternoon,
whispers urgent in the ear, of being called
from sleep by dawn's insistent touch to rise
only to love, only to live again.

THE LOVE-TALKER

after Ethna Carbery

O Mother, in the moonless land he came from
it wasn't the custom to travel with shadows—
he came alone and unannounced,

though as he walked the grass shivered.
As we lay on the ground, my weight stuttering
above his, we made no impression.

Though his lips were swollen and blue
his eyes burned their message into my flesh.
Mother, you'd have unbuttoned yourself to him

as readily as I, had he spoken to you;
you'd have seen Father's form grown young again
in the eloquence of his flat belly

and heaving sinewy back. As we lay together,
limbs tangled, no bird sang, no cattle moaned—
a numbing mist drifted about us.

Later, plaiting a wreath of bean leaves in my hair,
teasing my breasts with corn tassels and compliments,
he sang that I hadn't long to live.

I must leave now, Mother, Father—
my steps will leave no prints, my flesh no scents;
your daughter, you can tell your friends, has died.

To take away my home forever, hang scissors
above my bed, on my books and pillow
sprinkle churchyard mold, glass from a cracked mirror;

hang garlic and verbena from the necks
of the little ones before this long night—
I've a taste for words, a lust for conversation.

KNOTS

To purchase wisdom,
find a toothless old fisherman
wearing a shirt many sizes
too large tucked into pants
held up with a frayed rope
who'll offer to sell you
the wind in a knotted handerchief;
pay him whatever he asks.

To make someone yours forever,
fashion a doll in that one's image;
with string, bind its hands;
with string, hobble it.
Bare your teeth at the doll;
try to speak of love as you
bite off each knot's end.

When you've learned
to tie three knots in
the stream of water
falling from an overturned glass
you'll be too wise
for any guilt, too quick
to use your hands to sin.

HAZEL

To eat of the fruit
of this miracle's to become
the wisest of beings;
to feast on a salmon
who's feasted on hazel nuts
is to grow potent,
eloquent and fish-wise.

Hazel wands cut on St. John's Eve
by a bandy-legged virgin
of the true faith
will grow into divining rods
always thirsty, always
sending their palsy back up the arm.
A hazel rod held by an innocent hand
in black water near a child molester
will squeal like a pig.

Hazel twigs woven
into a wishing cap
and worn as a crown of thorns
during Lent, wedding night
or self-abuse will resurrect
the flame of need or bark of joy
in a life grown withered,
a form grown limp.

TO GROW HOLY

Chant your first three lies.
Remembering the gamble your parents took
to bring you here from where you were,
try to recall all that took place
before you were dipped in water.

For seven days and nights
using only your hands
keep the harvest moon
pastured in an autumn pond.

Kiss and kiss again the lips and limbs
of a woman love's never given pain:
if she pleads with you to stop, say you can't;
if she pleads with you not to, say you must.

On the shortest summer night
of your first year without parents
take your lover
to sleep unclothed in the unshorn grass
of a country churchyard.
At dawn, rows of stone leaning to shade you
from the moon
make a cross of your bodies and sing.

Think it unimportant when your wife
glances back at other men,
when you see in your child's eye
the one you'll never be.

Whistle during eulogies.
Tell nothing but the truth about the dead.

THE VIGIL: A FOLK TALE

On the eve
of every Christmas
for as long as even
the old ones can remember
the half-skeletons
that were once soldiers
ambushed by night
revive below the quiet field
alongside the old stone church,
claw their way out of the soil
that seals their eyes and takes
their breath away,
make gestures and speeches,
curse, skirmish and wage war.

Huddled in their pews
as the shimmer of incense and bell
drifts across the sanctuary
the villagers hear beyond stone
and God and crimson glass
the screams of their sons
mad to be dead again.

LAST RITES

1.

When death dances in,
tap-shoes rattling like dice
on the floor of your room,
assure him there's been no mistake;
ask if you may borrow
his faded straw hat, his grin.
Ask if you may lead;
waltz him out the door.

2.

Stake your claim early
to a plot of bright earth.
Break ground at dawn, sowing
the seeds your father left unplanted;
reap a future in crisp green bunches.
At the close of the harvest day
lie down in the soil, head to the east,
the ancient scent rising all around.
As the sun falls from the edge of earth
let the darkness race across your body.

FOUR : THE TRIAL OF MARTHA CARRIER

THE TRIAL OF MARTHA CARRIER

Several of her own children had frankly and fully confessed not only that they were witches themselves, but that this, their mother, had made them so. —Cotton Mather

She had a face that could kill a cow
or knock a man down at fifty paces.
She could, that rampant hag,
by touching a finger
to the side of the insult
that was her nose, chill
the brightest family hearth to ash and feud.

> *This Thursday last did I see*
> *yon hag consort in a sty*
> *with two swine—*
> *transform them*
> *into comely young men,*
> *fondle them as they*
> *took supper in the mud,*
> *the three of them*
> *erupting into cackles*
> *in the still night.*

At her command, it was testified,
the mating dance of swans
exploded before the eyes of children
into twitching rape.
Fathers heard ignorance in the words
of their sons; sons read lust
or failure in a father's face.

Wounds that smiled wide enough
to admit four inches of knitting needle
were, upon her being seized,

closed with a wet kiss.
Drinking wine, chewing flesh
in the forest dark
she was queen of hell, heiress to all,
a smiling harlot for a succession
of armies, intercessor and confessor,
every infant's fear and mother;

declared the most human,
the beast of beauty,
a little flower of evil.

WALT WHITMAN IN NEW ORLEANS, 1848

It's spring, moisture's
everywhere, blotting its signature
into hatband and shirtsleeve, cooling
each humid breeze, trickling
down the wrist to soften my palms,
these old oaks steaming,
whiskered with moss and dew.

Dark skin glistens in gaslight
as I pass; satiny pastels, lips
puffy with what they've known,
the secrecy of carriages, stifling rooms
strewn with clothing, glassy stares
in dim doorways, men kneeling
before women as if in prayer, women
to men, to one another, celebrating
the rain and blood and need
bending us toward the sea-breeze,
making us want to embrace
and move together forever.

At dusk, too many languages
and one language, scent of strange food
in pungent sauces, faint cries
and gasp of surprise—the world
aroused, all young men
old enough, waking suddenly
with something to say.

THE ANALYSIS

I existed frequently without a stomach; I expressly told the attendant . . . I could not eat because I had no stomach.—Daniel Paul Schreber

Yes there was a visitor again last night
but whether it was an incubus or succubus
I can't tell until you tell me who I am.

It began, Doktor, last Mother's Day
with the customary denial of paternity.

Russians and Poles in one-man subs
make daring night raids into my testicles.

Thin people the world over
are engaged in a conspiracy to eat
at my marrow until I too
am thin and conspiratorial.

Can I enjoy any meal knowing as I do
that three times each day all mothers
become larger?

My nerves before meals exalt themselves so loudly
they mingle with the nerve of God: cell and ganglion,
synapse, axon, dendrite, dynamo.

Yes! And radio interference
from the planet Venus, Israel and the Vatican.

36

Each night I stumble from
my aged wife's bed, my feet swollen big
as tombstones, the riddle of the sphinx
in my pajamas.

My parents employ earwigs and termites
to sabotage the wires inside my head.

She's wonderfully aggressive in a way
I wasn't born to be, her teeth are relics.

When self splits as I so often do into man and not-man
the partners embrace—this is holy love

and I love myself to watch me love one
another in others' eyes and mirrors
under God's approving rays

his energy a cancer in my soul

his love my downfall and rising

tearing apart to make me whole.

PARNELL

You would never have got young men to sacrifice themselves for so unlucky a country as Ireland only that they pictured her as a woman.—Charles Stewart Parnell

In the Queen's cellar at Eltham
the alchemist broods over books
on mechanical engineering, mining,
delivers painful speeches to spiders
in an American voice thin as ringing silver,
amplified by a mother's hatred
of antecedence and peasants.

A lord too shy to collect his rents,
he shocks a ghostly country with
wild superstition:
Beware of 13. Wear Nothing Green.
Blinded in Kilkenny, leading
a squad of goons to buy back
United Ireland, he dreams himself
sleepwalking into her room,
takes Healy's hand and calls him "Son."

He sleeps soundly on that last passage
from Holyhead to Kingstown pier,
wakes in time to accept a wreath
from his red-headed mistake.
"He's living," the red cabmen whisper
beyond the dark of Michan's, seeing
new lights in a troubled sky.

Pigott's letter, Carey's Irish sin
never touched you, lover:
but your mother going up in flame,
a country that slept with other men;
killed by contradiction, by what
you needed, what needed you.

THE DEATH OF RAY CHAPMAN

He was the best friend I had.—Tris Speaker

Carl Mays had hit five batters
that summer of 1920, and now on the mound
in a Polo Grounds' fog he counted slowly to 6.

Chapman dug in, bat near his head, and leaned
toward the plate, "the best bunter in the A.L.,"
they said later to be kind; but though his hands
were slow his arm was young enough to knock down
a runner from the back of the hole.

Mays' submarine toss submerged into mist
around home to surface at the side of the boy's head,
shattering the nerves that manage speech.
Chappie went down like a Texas Leaguer
plummeting between outfielders.

Muddy Ruel tore off the mask, sprang to his feet
and pivoted on the blood-ball, wheeling
to throw toward first. In Cleveland that night
downtown grew lurid with bonfire, thousands
cheered for Mays' blood, shook the cathedral
with the hands and feet of their prayer.

That fall Chicago went to hell in dark socks
and Cleveland ruled the world.

GRYNSZPAN, 1938

November in Paris:
a teenage Jew who loved the sound he made
when he prayed his name
and wanted all the world to be moved
by such fine singing
waltzed into the German Embassy,
a pistol sweating in his fist,
and spun around in a shower
of paperwork and spectacles
a small envoy of the Reich who hated
his father but bowed one time too many.
Just seventeen years from silence, eyes
crystal, teeth clenched tight, tendon and sinew
twitching in rigid columns,
he sang his Polish curses as the trigger
snapped back away from him and flesh
collapsed around the dark and dark
around the flesh.

In Germany two nights later, Dr. Goebbels
smiles beneath a twisted cross
at the cadenced schemes his fingernails drum out
along the tabletop, rattles his broken foot
to all the discord that has been and will be,
twenty thousand city souls danced into forest,
burghers prancing in the street below
to the lumbering polka of stone
and tears and shattered glass.

EZRA POUND IN ROME, DECEMBER 7, 1941: NOTES FOR A RADIO BROADCAST

It is not that I am a crank.

Damn it all O my America I'm no traitor either!
Roosevelt and his bankers made this war, made all wars—
not Spengler   not Il Duce   not Adolf

If presidents, popes and bureaucrats read Mencius, listened
to Vivaldi . . . . If all leaders cared as Jefferson, Van Buren
and Dante did about reforming their currency . . . .

You Allies misunderstand:
a gang of punks and bank pimps now rules England, the truth
of Aristotle, Hume and Saint Ambrose suppressed, Christianity
tainted by insane semitics, the American people too hog lazy
to examine the facts, an Occident scared out of its
nether garments by anything likely to cause thought . . . .

On the Axis turns the world of Art—
D'Annunzio acts while American scholars
make concordances to *Hiawatha*.

Divertente, Mussolini whispered when he'd read the Cantos,
entertaining, which proves my stuff appeals to men of action,
and Jesus Christ Almighty he's one! (I paper my office
with the Boss's face.) The Lincoln Brigade may not know it,
but Ethiopia's better off.

The League of Nations? Purest buncombe! By Rothschild
bankrolled! Morgenthau! Baruch! If a man has no order
within there'll be none without him. Confucius knew.

I've kept Joyce and Possum from the poorhouse, made
them read; Hem and Williams, even Frost, when the usurers

would have gobbled 'em up—
Send the Sixty Kikes Who Started This War To St. Helena!

The purest products of America
                              go crazy?

The old men with beautiful manners
                              all gone?
                                   usura
                                   usura
                                   usura
Tonight the sea's wine-dark beyond Rapallo,
all times here singly this moment: painted aurochs
grazing on the wall of my cell, each typewriter key
the click of another age
                              unbolting

I unravel into remembering—my time, theirs, its:
Hueffer rolling on the floor, my *canzoni* in his hand,
Bertrans de Born dancing and huffing toward war,
the limbs of Osiris yet
                              ungathered

I found love in the plaintive whine of a troubadour,
Social Credit, the just price—the key to all mythology.
Christ Died Because He Tried To Bust A Racket!

Bah! Tired! Head. Hurts. Tonight of all nights.
The FBI listens carefully
                         (I lose my thread at times)

I've stepped into the cage my words made
        stepped into the vortex
              Thanks for listening
                    listening
                         (Silence)

UNDER THE VOLCANO

The cries which might be the groans of dying or the groans of love. —Malcolm Lowry

These treble gins and brandies
won't fill me up
when I'm not working—not even
after-shave and amytal.
Only mescal gets me too blind
to mind the man with the fatuous grin
and dark glasses who follows me
from cantina to cantina, always
at least one drink behind,
and so many words.
He's been seeing my wife
or spying for my father, or both.
He knows I once punched a horse to its knees
for laughing at my walk, and that I
watched my own hands, without permission,
crack a rabbit's spine, and may have,
as the dream says, killed a boy
for loving me.
Such guilt deserves great punishment.

Don't say I'm a shit
and take your drink to another table—
it's just that my mind won't work
when it should, won't quit when
to save me it must.
I've been given too much freedom.
In Sicily I watched peasant girls
eat live sparrows just to still their singing;
in Oaxaca two fawns screamed in the hotel kitchen
before dinner, a vulture roosted on my washbasin.

Even now five Mexican cops wait under the table
for me to sleep so they can pour
cognac and nembutal down my throat
and I can spend another month on all fours.
Even Random House sends its agents out
to trace me; if I'm caught
they'll make me talk.

Trust me, because when I was five
my brother showed me in the syphilis museum
on Paradise St. in Liverpool
what love can do to beauty and the sailor,
because I've learned there's nothing
you can't learn to fear.
I'm here to see you can't be too kind.

Between the sea and my great thirst
stands the volcano, always overdue,
seething even when it's cold.
The difference between you and me?
The shades and shapes I recognize in what you know
as darkness only, light.

MARIO LANZA DEFEATS LUCIANO PAVAROTTI IN A TENOR COMPETITION HELD ON A TURNTABLE IN MY FATHER'S LIVING ROOM

Selections
M'Appari; La donna è mobile; Celeste Aida; Vesti la giubba.

Range
Pavarotti, while unmistakably Italian and a great tenor,
can't match the range of Lanza, who, having fallen apart
into stereo after his death, now ranges wraith-like through
my father's mind, throaty and full, high-low as siren.

Class
Pavarotti's got class, takes lessons, kisses hands
and while singing in French sounds like he's singing in French.
Lanza's got no class at all, often drank pints of scotch
and chianti during four loud plates of pasta, touched
greasy lips to silk sleeve, perspired freely.

Size
Pavarotti looks, father says, "wide as he is tall."
Lanza, long dead and still, now most likely's raw cold bone,
thin and sere, insubstantial, thin black discs
twirling on a spindle.

Tragedy
Pavarotti lives, eats, bows, appears on television, while Lanza—
father often told us as we grew up sober, middle-class
and Catholic—Lanza, having been dressed in corsets
like some swollen crone during his most intimate love scenes,
finally ate himself to death in Hollywood, buffeted about
by shame and his great gifts, the veins
in his head and heart popping like flashbulbs.

Results

Pavarotti's good, but he's not dead. He can't sing to father
of his youth, a vast lovely war and the world in uniform,
a beauty dim and constant, the stumbling rush to age.

FIVE : SITUATIONS

SITUATION NO. 3: THE ROLLING SKULL

Having fashioned
what you couldn't accept
of your self and parents
into a figure your own size,
you call it "enemy"
and in a struggle,
during which you prove
to the world and your lover
your purity of heart
and the sinew of your courage,
you behead this new man
but the head becomes
a grinning skull
rolling after you in the dust,
follows you into your dwelling
when you try to rest
or lie with your lover,
grows wings and a tail
and slithers or flies
after you through mud,
water and sky, laughing as if
it knew you better
than anyone else.

How do you get away?

SITUATION NO. 5: THE FUNERAL

You fill the air
with the death of mother,
the rattle of the rosary falling
from her hand, the rattle in her throat.

You recite father's last words,
gruff and muffled in a hospital pillow.
Your breath becomes theirs, your face and voice.

You learn to pray.

We hear you, they say from where they are,
we understand. Light candles, they say.

Soon in every window a candle flame dances.
How will you keep them alive?
What will you sing about now?

SITUATION NO. 7: THE POISON LOVER

One night
deep in middle age
as your lecherous spirit
bucks and wings you into pleasure,
you discover
that your young lover's long body
harbors a bouquet of snakes,
that she or he's been bred
by your worst enemy
for the sole purpose
of congealing you
into the cold meat of age,
that in your limp nakedness
you're without amulet,
scapular, mojo, prayer.

What do you do?

SITUATION NO. 9: THE CORPOSANT

You wake at the end of night
young again, all things new:
the celebration of moonlight and wind
in the pine-tops, the kindness
between a sleeping lover's legs.

You walk out alone
over the fallow fields that ring your home
rubbing a stone big as a child's skull
and marred by a fossil or the harrow's tooth,
carrying in your pockets
the few relics you've decided
you can't leave to others.

You see your body
grown lovely as candlelight
or moonlit mist move out to walk
beside you, then change direction
to go off alone, a diminishing place
glowing with sculpted tissue—
the bones of the face and hands
a geometry precise enough
to make you cry.

Tell me, what's the difference now
between what's left of you
and dawn?

SITUATION NO. 13: CITY HALL

Tall in a top hat,
the mayor, who minutes before
was gunned down by urban terrorists,
hands you the key to a city
where no one can live.

You make no acceptance speech,
but grateful and bright
before the cameras
you place a long hard kiss
on the corpse's lips, pledge
your political patronage,
borrow his hat.

Having invested heavily in real estate
and social love, you set fire
to your own obsolete foundries,
open a chain of carry-outs
in marginal neighborhoods,
make plans to take your family
away to the suburbs.

You become the target
of random acts of inhumanity.
Even you no longer believe
your speeches. You notice
one morning in the mirror
a hint of corruption, the birth
of insolvency, blight and decay.

What's your next move?

SITUATION NO. 33: THE FEAST

You're told the ingredients
have been assembled: for the sake of love,
wine and bread, fennel, honey and leeks;
laurel and bay to represent
your political importance and way with words;
a sampling of fabulous beasts and birds.
Fruits and meats to symbolize labor;
salt, the apple and lamb.

You're told the entertainment
will consist of your slow dismemberment
to the pulse of bass drums,
the plodding cadence of Gregorian chant,
screams of your parents and children.

You're told it will hurt
like nothing else, but after it's over
your very best friends will take you
home with them and place you
on altars in the midst of music and yearning,
place you near fire, teach their children
to sing your name.

Do you accept?

SIX : THE LIFE OF A SAINT

THE MARTYR

Beauty caught her unaware.
When her legs grew long,
when she felt breasts
and patches of hair
she lapsed into sorrow,
ached to be left alone.
When her frantic parents
decreed she must marry
she obeyed, but when her husband,
swollen with the things
of this world, first kissed her
she sickened. God took him,
she knew, because
he wouldn't stop trying her.
She said that during the twelve years
she lived walled up in a cell
near the altar, squinting out
of the tiny window toward Mass,
two strong, clean archangels
were her constant companions,
folding her in their cloaks,
touching her with their wings.
After the trial the Emperor himself,
humbled before his women and priests,
tortured her sacred nakedness.
Sixteen centuries on, mythic
in layers of Roman cemetery,
her beauty was found intact,
preserved in its triumphant gore.

In time, she learned all there is to know
about love.

JANUARY 5: SIMEON STYLITES

Patron of those who climb
and endure their heights, instruct us,
your earthbound successors,
in the ways of holy loneliness.

Teach us to stand over and apart,
to view unimpeded a sky wild with
larks, hawks and planets, touching emperors
only by bowing our heads.

Too mad for any monastery, wearing
little, you rode your swaying pillar
through heaven's variable winds
for a life's last twenty years,

touching only lettuce leaves, flies
and familiar stone.
Your talent for getting away saved you
from us, from yourself.

FEBRUARY 1:
IGNATIUS, BISHOP AND MARTYR

Even now at the end,
the growls of the crowd fluttering
in my gut, my only fear's that,
reading my life some day
on your knees, when it seems
the state's every fang has settled
in your flesh and the screams
of those who need are too near
for you not to hear, you'll
think me too hungry for death.

Why has a man been, if
in being no more he startles
no one, showers no timid spectator
with blood, sends no shiver
up and down the spine? I believe:
let my faith double, become
the two hard beasts
who'll grind me up until, fine
as the dust of this loud arena,
purer for a moment than any man,
I'll rise, bread of a famished Christ.

May I please you all.
May the one who sent me here
make of me one good meal.

FEBRUARY 5: AGATHA

She was born of wealthy parents, but *her* only wealth, and her misfortune, was the ocean sway of her hips as she walked through the marketplace, the slow white length of ankle and thigh, her breasts rising from a steamy bath. A loud and fat government man swelled for her; softly, eyes cast low onto his animal skin rugs, she said "no." So he placed her in a brothel run by a woman named Aphrodisia—you know the type—and she stayed long enough to know the whispered given name of every local John. She'd sit alone each evening, legs crossed in prayer, as content as if she were reading to herself. She was bad for business. So, growing louder and darker, forgetting all protocol, eyes small beneath a corrugated forehead, he ordered that she be beaten with sticks, stretched out on the rack, kissed with the torch. Still she remained constant, refusing to love or hate him in the way he wished. He had her breasts cut off slowly as he watched, fists clenched. Later, while she sat alone in her cell weeping into the stained glass chapel formed by her slender hands and very little light, as she computed the value of what she'd lost and what she might gain, Peter floated in on a shaft of sunlight and returned them to her. Once again she was all woman. This pleased her. Four days later she was rolled naked over crackling coals and glowing shards of pottery. This proved too much for her.

She's patroness of bells, bread and of course, breasts. The dates of her birth and death aren't known, nor is her place of birth—though both Catania and Palermo claim her. We can accept with certainty nothing of her story, but what will our doubt cost us?

FEBRUARY 9:

APOLLONIA, VIRGIN AND MARTYR

Old one, empty-mouthed,
a gold tooth hanging from your necklace,
how are we to understand
your one saintly act, the leap
from a lusting pagan mob
into the very tongues of bonfire
wagging outside Alexandria,
sky and heaven rising all around you?

Surely it was an act of God,
which made your fall sinless and sensible,
a voyage for old ones everywhere
to make near the end
when teeth, resolution and speech
have deserted them.

Why else would you
have lunged at earth moments before
it was to be served up to you?
Why else?

FEBRUARY 18: THE SONG OF BERNADETTE

I'm an old woman now, shapeless
in this habit, cloistered from the crowds
whose shouts I once ordered into litany,
whose withered limbs and stained souls
I bathed with water drawn from a well
I found one day
by stumbling into a mountain trance.

Twenty-one years later
I've had my fill of intercession—
the blue veil she hid her face behind
now shredded and soiled
by marauding, briefcase-toting advocates,
soulless scholars shipped in
from Paris, Dublin and Rome, skeptic doctors

who listen to my heart and story,
certain I'm mad as hell or Saint Catherine;
journalists, decaying dowagers
and raptured nuns—all those who,
before I knelt to ask heaven for a sign,
wandered lost, prayed
to pictures, terra cotta statues.

Soon after I saw what I said I saw
in the hot loneliness of adolescence,
every girl ran home
to shout the mountains alive
with pieces of heaven, magic springs,
promises numbered on beads, accounts
of what the Virgin wears to miracles.

My small untruth gave many
reason to believe their failure was but
prelude, their poverty wealth enough
to ransom a body from the tomb,
the stone their loved ones lay beneath
bright with tears and flowers.
Who am I to say they're wrong?

MARCH 8: JOHN OF GOD

In order to draw humiliations upon himself, he acted as a madman.—Lives of the Saints

A mercenary who watched so many
Hungarians and Turks die he was willing
to give his wits to the man who wouldn't
stay dead, John careened through the streets
of Granada selling books and cures,
bellowing at the poor until their children
sent him fleeing in a whirlwind of pebbles.

They chained him into an asylum, hoping
the scourge of extremes would melt away
his private cold, chill his fervor
for seeing things that weren't there;
but each time he crossed himself
the iron links clashed into hymns
too loud to be tortured away.

So each dawn, cross on his shoulder,
the old soldier marched from his hospital
to the door of some sleepy, belching sinner,
a woman's warmth still fragrant
on his fingers, and falling on him
sobbed "O Sweet, O Virgin Jesu,
come to us and wash our hands."

He died blind on his knees, asking God
to explain to him the madness
of devising such elaborate ways
of putting an end to what he'd made.
Fearing he might return,
the women of Granada followed him to the tomb
with garlands of garlic and chant.

MARCH 10:

THE FORTY MARTYRS OF SEBASTEA

The cold in Armenia is very severe, especially in March when the
north wind rages.—Butler's Lives of the Saints

There's a simple loveliness in cold, strong enough
to move the phalanxed hearts of the state's best warriors.
I'm Meletios, youngest and most literate of the radicals
culled from the proud Thundering Legion, now ordered
by the governor to wait for God on this frozen pond.
I address these last words to all who come after, and feel
at one time or another a real impatience with death.

We've done what we've done to heat the world,
to ensure not one more life will seep away unfelt.
We've been lovers in the only real way, but now
it's too frigid for tears and conviction's dammed up in us
like the flow of winter river our ashes will be
scattered over to drift into reliquary and sewer.

We were forty until one, suddenly pliant again,
gave up his spirit, joining the jailers in a warm bath
where he died the twisted death of extremes and lost
his crown of ice; we were forty again when one guard
dreamed a horizon awake with angels shivering out hymns.
His was a baptism of fire as he rushed to touch us,
never again to let go, nearly melting us with enthusiasm.

Crouched in wind, my mother stands at the edge
of this frozen world, smiling at heaven, happy with
her son's stubborn success. I can't move toward her,
the numb beauty of what I've nearly done
seeps through me. I stand on water, resolute forever.
Naked, flesh a gentle blue the shade of heaven,

I fall into sleep.

OCTOBER 5: FRANCIS

He desired me to be a new simpleton in this world.

Once when one of the brothers
put his hand to money

Francis ordered him to carry it outside
on his tongue and place it

on the newest pile of ass dung
he could find. Francis cursed a pig

for walking with a lamb, damned the ants
for living just to gather food

and preached to birds who sat and stared
and shit their bugs and berries

on his robe each time they heard
the Holy Word. Francis learned his truths

from the moaning of the wind
through trees, and polkaed barefoot

through the fields and forests
to the secret music whispered there:

that everything's ever one, one's
never more or less.

THE LIFE OF A SAINT

Born of parents of no real
piety—a couple who loudly enjoyed
his conception—he lived a youth
of pungent dissoluteness,
imaginative combinations of pleasure.
He spent much time in the company
of mirrors and minors, and it's said
that early on he went both ways.

Just before the horny, hairy
Visigoths disembowled every man and child
in his city, he painted his eyes and toenails,
then pleased his raucous captors,
dancing well enough
to delay his final glory.

His death, inflicted after
an unimaginative parade of tortures
with the usual devices was,
a minor chronicler reported, barely
worth mentioning. As for relics,
slivers of his shins will bring
no indulgence—his death
was as final as they come.

SEVEN : WHERE NO SON CAN EVER DIE

IN ANOTHER PLACE

Life breeds, of course it does;
our wry disguise of smile arouses
in bed or mirror the pleasant weight
to want, need's touch and squeeze
in place of sleep,

while in another place, slow
as maples bleed or dawn succumbs,
our parents, laughing loud, stop
and clutch their chests and,
falling, go away.

SPIRAL

A spiral ends
in what follows fury,
a storm in the calm
that spawned it, a life
in the culminating rage
whirling souls exhale,
as when your father
on a bed, the angrier,
grizzled you, his face
three circles of surprise
within a circle, rotates
slowly into dawn, pulling
on your hand long after
he's gone.

WHERE NO SON CAN EVER DIE

Crying "mother, mother,"
small men with jaguar faces
rope and stake her legs apart,
bind her close to earth.
She lies soothed and blistered
by night and day, centuries
stumbling from her, each breast
a mountain rising to heaven,
hair dense as jungle.
As she writhes, music bubbles
from her lips, earth quakes.
"It hurts," she whispers.

Each moan becomes in time
a pink and perfect child,
until she's become too old
to groan and roll in love
and its consequence,
and her grinning skull
becomes a temple
where priests scurry about
like spiders and ants,
where candles twitter like stars,
where no son can ever die.

TWO SCHOOLS

To say "my father speaks
in the dark voice of the forest beast,
flicks his lizard's tail
in and out of my dreams"
is to begin the same poem
written by Aesop and Ovid.

To say instead "my father
buys and sells chemicals,
copper and feldspar"
is to feel the room kick
and spin within you, gather
momentum like a locomotive;
or know the jump of air
and steaming rain,
the absolute peace
that follows confession,
an echo of love:
you wound the beast.

COMING OF AGE

A young man who last night
in the forest that rings the city
in his father's car
with burning fingers
touched a girl in three places
he never knew before
climbs at dawn
the stairs to the attic
of the only house he's known,
still dressed in the clothes
he wore as a child.
He finds his first bed
gray with dust, wooden bars
that segmented his days,
barred the light with shadow,
held him before he knew
the difference
between sunset and rising.

Alone, holding one small candle,
he marches around the crib
chanting his parents' names,
singing
       Ave maris stella,
       Dei mater alma.
He knows no one can harm him
as long as he remembers

the words and melody, knows
there's time until they'll come
to put him to bed for good.
When the candle's melted
over his hands already damp
from his first tears as a man,
leaving them smooth again
as a baby's,
the attic's black as night,
it's time for him to come down.

NIGHT JOURNEY

A man clothed in memories
that no longer fit him well,
his hair stained gray,
decides to return.

He rids the bedroom
of all light but his own
while singing softly
"On This Day O Beautiful Mother."

He sees her standing in the window
looking as he knows she looked
on the moon-bright night
his father knew her.

Her lips are moving, he hears
the Angelus prayers
inside his head, remembers
being gently bathed and fed.

Now he's ready to be old.

THE GAME

His hairy arms riding the chair
back and forth in front of
the sticky kitchen table,
father begins, having mastered
his face into an appropriate
category of grief: "enlarged
prostate," he baritones
across the wide table.

Mother, clearly hurt,
manages a feeble "cancer
of the cervix," falters out
a quiet "hysterectomy."
Defeat insinuates itself
between her tired eyes

and he knows he's won,
reaches to embrace her in
magnanimous arms, whispers
into her hair "myocardial
infarction, St. Vitus' dance,
gout, gout, gout."

THE WEEKEND

My father wants me to know
how happy he was
in the Solomon Islands in 1943,
how filled with passion
for his dainty Slovak bride,
to show me in the window of his face
how the chemical company hurt him
with a forty-three-year pain.

I'm reading his life
in the Lincoln H.S. *Log:* it says
he'll grow to be a purchasing agent,
former member of the Cleveland Singers' Club,
a lieutenant in the Catholic War Veterans,
Ascension of Our Lord Post.

There are times I feel I had
no father, but swam upstream on my
own initiative
toward an egg of light.
Other times, when shaving or writing,
I reach across the marriage bed
of the Columbus Fort Hays Hotel
or the Cleveland Statler
to brush with tentative lips
my mother's generous hair.

How could she leave me for him,
or he for her?

For the moments together it gave us
I love the Second World War.

EIGHT: THE THING

SCAPEGOAT POEM

You've long been guilty
of a deliberate callousness.

You're directly responsible
for the birds of decay
that flock in our cities.
Because of you
our old ones are desolate and brittle,
our children wild and untiring
in their pursuit of pleasure,
our industry obsolete.

A tide of blood's risen
with your sudden rise in the world.
Hysterical victims, their skin
burned, cut or soiled, hands
wild in their hair, accuse you,
point you out where you stand
on a stage with many others.

You've tried to intimidate
our young boys and girls, thrill
them into soiling themselves
with contempt for us; moreover,
we hold you responsible
for the curse of competition
flowering on our altars,
the bloodloving gods
we worship all the way to war.

You're the reason we can no longer
feel and sleep—there's
no one else to blame.

PREPARING TO LEAVE, HE ADDRESSES
THE CROWD THROUGH AN INTERPRETER

Thank you, he says,
thank you all for being here on time
to see him off on such an unpleasant day
in an age imprecise as this one,
when armies and governments seem
the only ones who plot by map or clock.

He knew your parents well, he says,
and feels the resemblance between them and you
most uncanny and more than a little unsettling,
settling as he is into age and regret.
(He hints in the nuance of his ancient tongue
that at one time a liaison might have been forged
between each of your mothers and himself,
but, he hastens to add, his pure love
for your fathers prevented him
from carrying through with those overtures
too overt to be misinterpreted.)
Your mothers were the flowers of youth,
he sighs, irreproachable, had soft cool hands,
eyes that contracted with anger in moonlight,
grew round in surprise and joy.

He wants you all to understand
he considers you the daughters and sons
he never had. His heart grows heavy:
he holds you dear and knows that where
he's going there can be no love but what
he brings, no heat unless he burns.

THE BALLAD SINGERS

Homeless Paddy and Mick
lean against one another
and against a burnished bar
somewhere below the border,
having fled Derry moments before
the ticking car they left
hurled two Orangemen in flames
thirty feet over the street.
The old soldiers conjure up
the faceless, motherless ones
blown apart by Michael Collins
because of Cromwell.

As the laughter of heroes
bubbles up from their dark pints
the old ones, pure spirit now,
slip from their nests of flesh
and circle the room to bursts
of remembered music: pikes
and harps mirroring moonlight,
a rifle bright as a lover's eye,
bold gallows speeches, shattered
knees, the tattoo and siren
of the Thompson and the pipe—
green fields fading to black and tan.

THE LESSON

Never look away
from grounders; never
retreat, hoping for a good hop.
If shattering and pain are on the way,
better to measure them first.

Learn to read the bias
of the curve, the pitcher's wrist
snapping down as if the hand held
a flaming match too long.
No failure burns like his

who turns to kiss the dust
wide-eyed as the sphere
veers to smack leather
between the neck and groin
of the smiling, prescient catcher.

No sins invite retribution
like missing the cut-off man,
walking a myopic pitcher, smirking
at coaches, owners or age—
when seasons are reckoned

errors become your name.

MIDDLE LINEBACKER

Following instructions willed me
by my big-bellied gray teachers,
I keep my shoulders parallel
to the yard lines. I won't move
before you do, so I'm always
a step behind, but I'm a wizard
of angles. Sudden change sickens me,
and pain ends only when confusion
does, when we hide in the impact
as if it were a forest, lie together
in chalk and clipped grass.

My hands are nets, my arms
oak and ash, wound like a mummy's.
Through holes in my skull voices harsh
as stones chant, cry out in numbers
and prediction, pleas for help.

Later tonight, fear forgotten
or tinged with the myth time makes
of things that don't quite measure up,
our laughter will flow around the table.
Now, those here with me are lost,
gather around like calves, ache
for a future. I'm no seer.
I've been so wrong before

my bones have rattled, lungs
have groaned like thunder. But once
you've decided and your courage
and momentum meet just outside your body
I'll be there crouching in your way,
brushing aside your friends as if
they were twigs.

I'll pound you into the ground
like a stake.

THE FARMER

"Here's the latest now
from heaven and Nashville," he lisps.
He broadcasts daily from station WRFD.
Crouching low on a three-legged stool,
gripping the mike he breathes out
five-minute market and weather reports,
testimony on religion and combines:
    "I run my John Deere
    on the power of the Lamb's Blood.
    Each green shoot shouting
    in my contoured fields praises
    the name of Jesus and his Daddy.
    My field corn walks about
    in the holy wind, strutting
    with joy and wonder, soybeans
    speak in tongues, pigweeds
    roll over dead when they hear
    the Holy Word. My chickens
    die of happiness, convinced
    their time's come, necks rent
    by the marvelous power.
    Black Angus somersault into air,
    click their hooves, bellow
    'Lord God of Hosts.'
    In my orchard grow apples
    untasted, moaning for the worm.
    It's good to be a farmer."

ASTHMA

Rattle the drums,
blow short bursts on the horns.
I like the noise, feed on confusion,
thrive on what's all too human.
When you've forgotten the sound
of a clear sigh I'm there to remind.
When you're walking through autumn
I'm winter, the brittle branches
of my fingers scraping across your chest
when the wind blows.
I'll steal your lungs,
breathe with them at my own
slow pace. Show you fear me
and I'll grow like a weed.
I'll kiss your children on the mouth
when the sun sets and again at dawn.
I pile your chest with weights
ponderous as churchyard monuments,
change your dreams of tomorrow
into pleas for every breath.
Run to the telephone,
hide in clouds of steam, bottles
of bitter pills. I'll be here,
never farther from you than your doubt.
You can't run—I've got you chained
to earth at the edge of the sea;
the roaring you hear's
the onrushing tide.

THE BED

All day long you neglect me, sugar.
All night we wrestle. My voice
would be the song your body'd sing
if gravity's fist unclenched. (Jesus
that's poetic!) I'll be a dumb blonde
for you, squeal each time you move.
Naughty boy, you cover me
in shrouds of long white. You could
ride me anywhere. I'd take every inch
of you, croon about how big you are,
how close you are to tearing me apart
with your magic fury. I'd spit out
what you're doing to me
in foul words in four languages.
We'd lie here at night
and dream each other, if only
you'd cooperate. Relax, let your body
meet mine. I'm no cackling witch,
just a mouth without your mother's teeth.
Last night I heard you whisper to yourself,
mumble like rain on the oak leaves beyond
our wall. I'm an angel, baby, come
to save you from your solitude,
your coiled body steady in my palm.
I'll never let you down. Let me tell you
what happened between me and my best
girl friend one night when I was thirteen.
You'd like that, wouldn't you?

ROOSTER, PIG, DOG AND JAGUAR

He's become domesticated.
To keep the heat away he wears
shirts, builds a small house
to hold back the jungle, lives
in shadow and peace with the animals
he's come to know: lust he calls
Rooster; his stupidity, Pig;
anger he names Dog.

But in his mind the Jaguar,
insistent as memory, struggles,
hurls itself in desperation against
skull walls smooth as ivory.
The shock of its screams, like
some great wind but greater because
it comes from inside, pitches him
back and forth against the columns
of trembling house until there's
no balance, no middle or shade,
only dim red heat behind the eyes,
dull drumbeat of pulse,
bared snarl and fang, the grunt
of the body shattering walls.

The pain in his eyes scalds.
His own tropical music dances him
back to jungle, the family of beasts.

THE THING

Rubbing her back and legs
he raised sparks of rapid breath
and beads of moisture. Everything
in the car was soft with dew; their mouths
fell into each other. They lost their minds
in adolescent desperation.
It was natural then, that, the radio being off,
they wouldn't have heard
of the thing's glowing arrival,
its landing in a nearby forest, reports
of unspeakable horrors, its thirst for innocent flesh.
When the car began to rock he thought
it was her sixteen-year-old happiness
moving below him; the odor
he gave to her as well. She thought,
seeing it all at once framed in the passenger window,
that it looked desperately like his mother;
he, that it bore a ferocity akin only
to her father. Their final seconds were spent
together in fright and clasping,
locked in one another's limbs,
the evidence of passion thick on the windshield,
part of something they couldn't stop.
It would be left to someone else
to call out the army, the wise men in white coats
who'd try to still this thing
with electricity or bacteria or fire
or kindness. They lay together
in the dark belly of a piece of night sky,
stilled for all time,
out of the picture, safe again.